I0108622

UNTITLED

A COLLECTION OF THOUGHTS, POEMS, & REFLECTIONS

ZACHARY X. ALLAN

Copyright © 2017 by Zachary X. Allan

UNTITLED

All rights reserved. This book or any portion thereof
may not be reproduced or used in any manner whatsoever
without the express written permission of the publisher
except for the use of brief quotations in a book review.

Printed in the United States of America

First Printing, 2017

TABLE OF CONTENTS

CHAPTER II. LOVE, LUST, & LOSS 21

CHAPTER IV. GROWING PAINS   73

EPILOGUE

PROLOGUE

Untitled. A book for those who know me, knew me,
grew with me, shaped me, triggered a thought, or
sparked an emotion. A book for those of you who
have touched my heart. Whether you know it or
not, you are my daily inspiration. So, embark
on this journey with me and find yourself inside
this piece of my mind on paper. I can only hope
this book touches and inspires as many people as
have done so for me.

-thank you-

CHAPTER I

THE ENIGMAS OF LIFE

"words have no power to impress the mind without
the exquisite horror of their reality"

-Edgar Allen Poe-

SELF REFLECTION

Living life can be some heavy shit sometimes.
So remember, your happiness in life depends on
the quality of your thoughts. Everything as we
know it has a pulse; choose to be alive with
it! Everything affects everything through the
ripples of life. You may not know yet where it
is you belong or where you are going.
So, let that be forgotten and allow yourself
to embrace your inner weird. You no longer need
permission to live life the way you want to.

The meaning of life is defined by what you allow
to mean something. It is correlated with what
you value. You have control. Your priorities
will speak for themselves through actions and
time. These are the few things I am sure of. As
for the rest of life, it will entwine itself
within what you attract, how you think, and who
you desire to become.

INSPIRATION

the daily interaction
stimulus that keeps
me ticking
the renewable inspiration
daily actions
i keep kicking
the fundamentals of caring
the art of interaction
the enigma of fate
this is what sustains
the hunger i have
to create

CHAPTER I

WILD BLUE YONDER

i will write
until my throat bleeds
screaming words onto paper
i will live
until my mind no longer wanders
grasping at my ever drifting consciousness

UNTITLED4

i'm your **BIGGEST** problem and *only* solution
i don't know what to say or do
all i'm capable of is thinking of you
we all have that certain someone or something
who or what is it for you?

ANXIETY

the looming indefinite
something that seems to be your shadow
not always present
dropping in without notice
it follows you
you seek shelter in the dark
the bottle
the pipe
the pill
no matter the suppressant
it always returns from hiding
you will do anything to ease your anxiety
but it's all temporary
you cannot cure it
you cannot run from it
it is everpresent
what do you seek?
peace of mind?
reassurance?
relief?
your greatest weapon lies between your ears
your greatest vice-your understanding
your only armour
recognizing its existence

"SURE"

it screams complacency
it screams indifference

i hate it

it isn't yes
it isn't no
it isn't anything

do you care?
"*sure*"

<u>BEING BLUNT</u>

as others
dodge and evade honesty
i beg you
be blunt
i can't afford anything else
my feelings can't handle it
my head can't comprehend it

the opposition is no longer satisfactory
i don't have time for it
let your voice be heard
express your emotions
be blunt

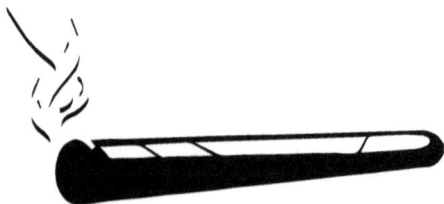

HEAVEN

paint me a mind picture
with your words
one that i can feel

let reality be so vivid
my neurotransmitters surge
i feel my thoughts and see my future

no action too large
no thought inconceivable
all is possible
everything is connected
i am here

HELL

imagine if
all the things most important to us
were not gone
were not dead
but worse
had never happened

UNTITLED

MELANCHOLY MINDSET

sometimes, i like being sad
a mildly comforting reminder
i am real

sometimes, i think to myself
maybe if i'm sad
sad enough, long enough,
something's bound to make me happy eventually

-"*that's how it's supposed to work, right?*"-

DIET OF THE MIND

you must keep feeding your nightmares
in order for them to survive
your acknowledgement
is their life line

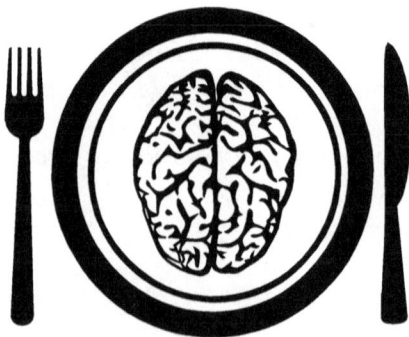

SUPERNOVA

the infinite universe
contracts and expands
gasping for air

our ego
the tar on her lungs
our greed
her tumour
no longer benign

our compulsive expansion
denying her breath
we need, we want
the excess of our lives
is the end of hers

the personification of a black hole
society, the supernova
we consume ourselves

LOCATION

when your mind wanders
as mine does often
do not worry
regardless of where
or how far your mind takes you
you are where your feet are

WHITE BLANK PAGE

sometimes i feel lonely
even in good company
so i turn the page
write another line

the blank facade of an endless white landscape
is the only thing to take notice

offering an open ear
no matter the circumstance
it listens
hugging my words endearingly
as the ink soaks through
its porous skin

<u>1(800) 273-8255</u>

"how's it going"
he casually asked as i walked by

"it's going"
i murmured without breaking stride

"that's better than stopping"
he replies

i hesitated just momentarily
while taking my next step

i heard sincerity nor sarcasm in his voice
and although he may not know it
he just saved my life

NEWTON'S FIRST LAW

i cannot comprehend
the adversity you may face
but a brilliant mind once told us
it's easier to just keep going

-an object at rest stays at rest
an object in motion stays in motion-

MY ILL MIND

i need you
i want you
i love you

but before you can do the same
wander into my ill mind
then tell me

do you need me?
do you want me?
do you love me?

DEATH'S DOOR

bury me amongst the trees
the leaves
and let me rot

let my soul decompose
let my body transpose

open the old wooden door
break the brittle brick of reality

and

let me ascend
to what we know and think of
as the end

'TIL DEATH DO US PART

It's uncanny how complicated people make it to
see the simplest beauty in life. I too fell into
this void, believing everything was a tragedy.
Over time I evolved into someone who can
appreciate the tribulations of life; what were
once tragedies are now the beauty that drowns my
fears in waves of hope.

CHAPTER II

LOVE, LUST, & LOSS

"it's only in the mysterious equation of love
that any logical reasons can be found"

-John Nash-

THE FLUME OF LOVE

Sometimes, in order to love someone in a new
light, in a new way, we must first let them go.
It is okay to be alone. Learn from yourself,
discover what you value, and explore where your
morals lie. Truly find yourself, alone, just you.
Be frightened, heartbroken, mournful, jubilant,
content, but most importantly, immerse yourself
in life. See the potential around you and follow
your head and your heart simultaneously as you
persist precariously.

FOUR LETTERS

love is a word
with a million meanings

all you have to do
is give it one

<u>DECREPIT LOVE</u>

you had problems
i did too

i wanted to help
but could not rescue you

that's the ending
that's the sad thing

that we couldn't finish
the beginning

BALANCE

art is the delicate balance between knowing
what's a masterpiece
and when to stop the stroke of your brush

similar is love
when do we spread our love?
when do we paint the last line

finding the balance is the beauty in both
finding the balance is impossible
like art, love is always left for interpretation

BEAUTY

it is not your shell
it is not your facade

your foundation of beauty
is built upon

your generosity
your intelligence
your compassion
your hospitality

this is where your beauty lies
this is your foundation
this is why i love you
this is what makes you lovable

SATURDAY'S SOLACE

you're the book i read
as i watch the storm roll in
soothing my world
with gentle words
and softer lips

you're an aromatic blend
of
love and comfort
complimented nicely
by cream and sugar

you're my cup of tea
on every rainy day
my solace
my empathy
my everything

DEAR VALENTINE

i don't mean to sound crazy
i can't afford to sound insane
i fear sounding needy

but

i just needed to tell you
i've thought about
spending the rest of my life with you

MUSCLE CRAMPS

my heart tightens
everytime
i see your face or hear your voice

muscle cramps
that won't go away

my heart tightens
everytime
i see your face or hear your voice
because
it's just as breathtaking as the first time we met

LOST AND FOUND

your attention i crave
all throughout the day

your company i need
my soul to feed

our time together bound
and somehow i feel lost
yet found

TRAPPED IN MY MIND

trapped in my mind
nowhere to hide

you broke my heart
i don't know where to start
i sat there and cried myself to sleep

then i leaned a little closer
felt your presence in my sheets
it was all a bad dream
i had just dozed off
learning from my fears
in this wonderful wasteland
between my ears

SOLITUDE IS BLISS

solitude is bliss
until you give me a kiss

remind me where i am

snuggled deep
between the sheets

where our love dwells

EXPIRATION DATE

from the second we met
our love had an expiration date
you told me from the beginning
that this would end
our worlds slowly separating
like chunks in curdled milk

from that moment

it was all i could think of
that soon enough
you would no longer be mine
i wanted you around
every second possible
i needed you all the time
because the future was certain
the expiration date was stamped on
our hearts
and the simple idea
that our love was inevitably broken
kept slowly tearing us apart

<u>QUESTIONS</u>

i feel so alone
like i can't breathe
i feel like i need to get up and leave
my destination unknown

and as we talk on the phone
you make me wonder
who am i?
where am i going?
my head and heart
start overflowing

my emotions are lost
i'm only thinking of you
i don't know if that's entirely true
i say "*i love you*"
but i question that too

USED

you used me
only when you needed me
because you knew you could
because i would always be there
waiting
dangling by a thread

you'd show up
just before i was about to let go
you used me
just enough to keep me attached

then cut me off
let me dangle in the wind
and wait
wondering
when will she come back?

<u>HOW THINGS ENDED UP</u>

i hate you
i hate how you make me feel love
although it is now unrequited

i hate how you use to make me smile
all the while i just sit and wallow
my soul, now hollow

i hate seeing
your new love growing
while i pass you two by
i'm wondering

why things ended up like this…

i hate myself
i hate how i gave you everything
my love unconditional

i hate how i could never make you smile
all the while
you thought i never cared
similarities
we never shared

i hate how i'm alone
no love to be seen

while i pass you two by
i'm wondering
why things ended up like this…

CONFUS(ED)ION

I struggle to comprehend your inability to
love me as much as I love(d)you

BOTH

they say that the last thing you think about
right before you go to sleep
and right when you wake up
are the source of your happiness or pain...
now that you've been both
i'm sitting here staring at this rope
do i tie it in a knot
do i choke
or do i change my perspective
like you did
make this all a joke
my happiness once revolved around you
that fucked me up
my sadness is because of you
now i'm really fucked up
my happiness is me
my sadness is me
i have control
but only now did i see
you're not good enough
you never were
i'm just impatient
that's what's killing me
i want to fall in love again
i want all of what i once had

<u>STRANGERS</u>

i wish i didn't know you
i wish we were strangers
not out of regret
not out of anger

i've longed to stumble
upon your soul
in hopes, just maybe
you'd make me whole

we'd meet anew
along our journeys

not having a clue

that this collision of fate
would give our love a new hue

CHAPTER II

TOGETHER

i simply can't imagine a world without you
but somehow
you can't imagine one with me

"KEYS-WALLET-PHONE"

i miss you
i miss you like i miss the simple things

i miss you like
the keys left in the locked car
in sight but impossibly out of reach

i miss you like
the purse forgotten in the shopping cart
necessary for functionality, but left behind
without second thought

i miss you like
the phone lost on the subway
abandoned on an empty seat as strangers pass by

i miss you because you were my
"keys-wallet-phone"
before i left home
but i've lost you
now i'm just alone
walking home
without my
"keys-wallet-phone"

<u>MOURNING ROUTINE</u>

she tastes like burnt coffee
sitting on my tongue
what was once
the start of my morning routine
now just a bad taste
left on the palate of my mind
too distinct to be forgotten
too bitter to enjoy

HOOKED

today i found that shiny hook
swinging from the trees
what it used to hold before it snapped
a million happy memories
today i found that shiny hook
rusted in the tree nook
the tree grew around it
until i found it
unaware of the memories it held
the past is where my mind dwelled
today i found that rusted hook
that held my confidence high
until you left me with your last goodbye
we'd laugh and play by the fire pit
you told me we were the perfect fit
while tarzan danced on the bed sheet
like the day i swept you off your feet
reminding me, nostalgia's so bitter sweet
today i saw that rusted hook
and ripped it off the tree
like removing memories
that will leave me scarred
reminiscing of what happened in that backyard

<u>SOMETIMES</u>

now, less frequent than often
i find myself thinking of you
as you mosey into my mind
disregarding how that might make me feel

i wonder

do i captivate her thoughts
when she's least expecting?
like she does for me

does she think of me anymore?
like i think of her

did she love me?
like i loved her

"probably not"

DISTANCE

it still hurts
to think of you
the only progress i've made
is to distance you

i've learned to think of you less
give
my
head
heart
and
emotions
a rest

LETTING YOU GO

letting you go
was the hardest thing
while i knew you'd hold on
by a string

but i couldn't burden you
you had better things to do
our love was smeared
i let you go
yet, you hover near

REALIZATION

i am no longer the person you once fell in love with
and for that
i will no longer apologize

HOPELESS ROMANTIC

i'm a hopeless romantic
with an outrageous need to give

i have trust issues
but i'm blindly loyal

this is why, often times
i find being alone
better than being lost

ALL OF THE ABOVE

you go out on a limb
to find that certain someone
surprised with what you will find
similarities and differences
you don't seem to mind

you long for their presence
like Adam did Eve
you'll dread each time
they unexpectedly leave

they're the sun
that helps you grow
when they're with you
time moves slow
then reality hits
when they've let you go

it's a magical thing
the human bond
whether it be friendship or love
it's about how we respond

we walk down this path
independent but together
wondering, pondering
about the storms that we've weathered

SOMEONE NEW

just waiting for someone new
to be that person
i think of

every day
every sunset
every sunrise
every sad encounter
every moment of joy

just waiting for someone new
to be my something,
all the time

to be my everything,
once again

GOLD STANDARD

i was so in love with you
that now
whenever i meet someone
someone new
you are the criteria
you are who i compare them to
you were my norm
now you're my standard

REGRET

we fucked
and you instantly regretted it
but for that moment

i was your clarity
your paradise

if

if i could be that for you
just for one moment
than the pain i face
the rejection i feel
will all be worth while

CUPCAKE PHASE

i dream of finding
that someone

to skip the bullshit
just dive in

to skip the fairy tale
just fall in love

UNTITLED2

love is a two way street
and often times
i find myself walking down an alleyway

CHAPTER III

PERPETUAL PERSPECTIVE

"everything we hear is an opinion, not a fact.
everything we see is a perspective, not the truth"

-Marcus Aurelius-

PERSPECTIVE

Often times our perspective on life is faced
outwards. What if instead of this we looked
inwards? Thought of ourselves and how others see
us? Or, what if we did neither? Can we? Is it
possible? Can we look around and refuse to stay
within the lines of in or out? Me or them? Am I
living in the world or is the world just theirs?
Am I an outsider?

Can we just live and experience moments as
a present from the present? Can we refuse
introspection and judgment? What do we call it?
Not focusing on things, people, or perspectives.
It's called the **NOW**. It's your greatest
renewable resource and is everpresent. It
depends simply on if we choose to see it, live
in it, or remain ignorant.

TOMORROW

you talk of tomorrow
as if it isn't already here

<u>UNTITLED1</u>

it's life
activities available
experiences accessible
just add meaning

EXPLORE

we lay wasted
in the wake of routine

we lay dreaming
in anticipation of adventure

two paths
one destination

the difference?
the journey

BE WHAT YOU MIGHT HAVE BEEN

imitation
merely a circumstance of
education
affection
culture

replication
merely a myth
no two interactions
can be perceived or impact reality
in the same way
for every action
the thoughts
perceptions and emotions
will be endlessly different

this is why
life is so incomprehensibly interesting
we cannot wrap our minds around it
but why try?

<u>A WAY OF TRAVEL</u>

life has countless beginnings
all things have an end
why is it that those are our focal points?

the lens through which we choose to see the world
is all that matters
the journey is where we spend our time
so why fret?

take endeavors with the return of the sun
figure life out on the run
experience without animosity
and live as if
happiness is a way of travel
not a destination

CHAPTER III

FOOL'S GOLD

don't
let the fool's gold
of reality
shred your soul

FORWARD

we fall
we fail

life brews with these inevitable encounters

whenever you fall
whenever you fail
go forward

5:47AM

in the past
my mind whispered to itself
faint reminders
of
who i was

right now
my mind bellows
with questions
of
who i am

someday
my mind will scream
with clarity
of
who i am becoming

<u>TODAY MY PROFESSOR TOLD ME</u>

we are made of the same basic compounds
found in stars
how outlandish

that twinkle in your eye
might be your soul

your shiny skin
might be peppered with star dust

that glistening smile
might be a nebula's reflection

your innocent giggle
might be an echo from space

today my professor told me I'm a star
that we all are

SPACE

sixteen times
the sun rises and sets
the man on the moon
forgets to rest

the unknown of space
so beautifully frightening
the knot in your heart
endlessly tightening

as you look down upon
what was once your entire existence
now
a fleeting nightmare

MEMORIES

reminisce of the past
that passed too fast

fleeting beauty

realities contrast
feelings so vast

perpetual pain

"I̲"

do not entrust too much hope
in humanity
but do not lose hope
all together
we all have our own agendas

no matter
how much
we try
how often
we care
how kind
we act

"I" always come first
and so do you

NEUTRAL

conflict feeds the soul
indifference kills it

being different causes chaos
yet garners sanity

contrast is the color of life
so why be neutral?

3:12AM

what we resist
persists indefinitely

what we let go
flows formerly

what we grow to be
eventually
someone's happiest memories

LIFE TO LIVING

art in my ears
philosophy between them

creation from my hands
action within them

life in me
love around me

action to reaction
thought to process
life to living

<u>SSENDAM EHT OT DOHTEM</u>

to think others can control you
is a horrible mistake
you do not need
permission to live

your experiences do not need to be categorized
explained
quantified
rationalized

these tragic routines
a way to make sense of reality?
somehow, it feels so fake
a cage to be broken
a mind to be freed

CHAPTER IV

GROWING PAINS

"in any given moment we have two options: to step
forward into growth or to step back into safety"

-Abraham Maslow-

<u>RECENTLY</u>

Over these past few months I have learned to
live in the **NOW**. Although it is not possible one
hundred percent of the time, it is necessary for
peace of mind. I've learned through experiences
(both beneficial and world shattering) that you
really never know what your last experience
with someone or something might be. Whether
it's a family member, friend, significant other,
stranger, hobby, or adventure it may very well be
your last experience or encounter with them/it.

Things happen, people change, emotions shift,
relationships alter, and adventures fade into
memories. Nothing is permanent, not even life
itself. Before you get out of bed this morning,
before you drink your coffee and set off on your
daily routine, I challenge you to make it your
intent to show gratitude and cherish all that
you experience and encounter as if it may never
happen again. You do not have to change your
lifestyle. Simply be cognizant and grateful for
everything, no matter it's outcome, as it serves
a purpose and has it's place in your journey.

CERTAINTY

everything is happening
exactly as it is supposed to
the universe does not make mistakes
of this
i am certain

RITUAL

"wake" /wāk/ - a vigil by the body
of a dead person before burial

i attended a wake this weekend
a young man passed too soon
his youthful death
seemed so inopportune

we met in preschool
years once long forgotten
now he's nineteen
as i approach his coffin

i walked down the aisle
to express my empathy
as stories of "just the other day"
were shared endlessly

he left us in a wake of love
the ripples have just begun
we celebrated his life
the ritual was done

IMPACT

"wake" /wāk/ - the path or course
of anything that has passed or preceded

your vessel of life
with a hole too big to be patched
your body's been buried
the soul no longer attached

we lay in the wake
of a life well lived
we mourn at your funeral
you were just a kid

the impact you've made
in a short nineteen years
a smile that changed lives
now brings us to tears

i was at your wake
and am in it too
your impact on my life
now feels brand new

<u>LIMITS</u>

what if we have limits
what if what they told us was a lie?
what if the glass ceiling was brick?

what if our timeline
was determined solely
by what we have to offer the universe?
maybe we can only give so much
it is not our health
that determines our demise

our heart
ego
soul
generosity
are the fabric of reality which
only we have control of

the universe knows
she bellows with certainty of our ability
the good die young
not because they didn't deserve more
but because they gave all they had

-gently running towards death-

A TRIP AROUND THE SUN

365 days
a turn in the world
a year of life
we see growth
we make change
a year in the present
a lifetime
a year in the past
a short memory
a year in the future
a big question
how does something have so many faces?
365 days
a turn in the world
a year of life
we sum up these memories
a story
told in minutes
actions compiled over time
into change
modification
transformation
growth
expansion
improvement
what a wonderfully frightening opportunity

GUTS

it's easy to go back
to what we knew
what once was comfort

but

it takes guts
to be patient, to make a future

TENSE
(Past-Present-Future)

these ghosts from the past
keep calling my name
these ghosts from the past
drive my head insane

that love i once had
it's scratching at my heart
that love i once had
it's pulling me apart

the future i see
is right in front of me
the future i see
could set my mind free

but the temptation it echoes
the temptation it screams
to fall back to where i once was
or live out my dreams

GROWING PAINS

with life comes love
with love comes pain
we associate pain with loss and defeat
but truthfully
pain is the greatest way to grow

TRANSITIONING

from the kid with all the friends
to the one who eats alone each meal

from the kid who hit that home run
to just another number on the roster

from the kid with the sexy girl
to the one who can't find someone steady

from the kid who had it all
to the kid who has nothing

from the kid that nobody understands
to the kid that finally gets himself

from the kid who's his own worst enemy
to the one who's his only companion

from the kid that people thought had everything
to the kid that has peace

i'm that kid who found himself
i'm that kid who's still searching

INVISIBLE LINE

it takes courage to put yourself second
to make life about others

it's a very fine line

between
selfishness and humanity

TWO JOBS

in life
we only have two jobs
to learn, and to cope

we must cope
with the tragedies we have learned of
we must learn
from the knowledge we have gained

UNTITLED3

found tranquility in chaos
and comfort in pain

PERSISTENCE

when in pursuit
of our greatest desires
we oftentimes hear
a million no's
before we hear
the yes we've been looking for
although you may falter
or second guess
do not stray
from the path you've set

NATURAL STRUCTURE

there is no end
only new beginnings

life isn't linear
growth is fluid

WHO ARE YOU?

Yes, I could be like you. I could be strict,
quiet, and formulated, but that's not me. That's
not who I am. I'm a clusterfuck of thoughts. I
leave my emotions abandoned on white, ink soaked
skin, and empty ears. I am not a pattern. I am
a mishmash of creatively logical and aimlessly
wandering. I'm the awkward stain on your lucky
shirt. You refuse to wash me away because
although unwanted, I too mean something to you.
I am an open book that echoes with depth and is
painted with vibrant diction. I'm in love with
life and fascinated by fate. I am an organized
mess and act on impulse more times than not.
I'm proof that life's worth living.

So, yes I could be like you, but why would I want
that?

"ZACK AND ALLAN"

Zack: the one with the experiences, the one living life, the one things happen to. Allan: the one who wanders through the streets of life late at night, occasionally stopping for a moment to take something in. Allan knows Zack from the classrooms and nine to five, seeing him go through the motions. Zack knows Allan from the darkest corners of his brain and the creative dissonance caused by their joint existence. They share their fondness of hourglasses, abstract art, vintage photography, the taste of bold coffee, and an articulate tongue; although these similarities are appreciated through an incomparable scope. Coexistence is crucial: we live, let each other go on living simultaneously, regardless of the circumstances.

Allan composes his ink on paper, and these words justify Zack's existence. The pages whisper, not with validation, but with confessions of hope, perspective, and reality. The white facade is not an effort to save one of us, but perhaps merely documentation of our shared realities. Nevertheless, one of us will perish indefinitely. This is the only way the other can survive. The slow game of tug of war is soon to come to an end. They give everything to each other as the grey lines of reality are blurred and bent with time.

Spinoza knew that all things long to persist in their being; the stone eternally wants to be a stone and the tiger a tiger. I shall remain in myself *-if it is true that I am someone-*. Through the untitled years and recognition of Zack and Allan I have tried to free them from myself. Therefore, my life is a flight, I lose everything, and everything belongs to the universe.

 -inspired by "Borges and I" by Jorge Luis Borges-

————————————.

only now
did you realize
that i've been talking to you directly

i'm in your head
as you read this very sentence
but that's the point

because

you're in my head too
this written word
UNTITLED
i now leave with you

EPILOGUE

Why title something *UNTITLED*? In my mind,
UNTITLED is an oxymoron, a bent perspective
folded in upon itself. The idea as a whole
fascinated me in some twisted way. While the
creation of this book began, I simultaneously
drafted a parallel idea...an alternate way
to read *UNTITLED*. By rereading "UNTITLED
1,2,3,4" and "_____." in this order, you can
experience an exclusive perspective and added
layer to this piece of my mind on paper. It's
UNTITLED, on a completely different timeline,
compressed into a story of it's own. A book
within a book. So, to finally answer my own
question...*UNTITLED*, is untitled for all of
the reasons you find along the way of reading
it. This book is a casual walk in the back of
my mind, an insight into
my reality and how I view the life I'm living.

With My Deepest Sincerity,
-thank you for being interested-

www.ingramcontent.com/pod-product-compliance
Lightning Source LLC
Chambersburg PA
CBHW072043040426
42447CB00012BB/2992